Catch Me
with
Your
Smile

Other books by

Blue Mountain Press INC.

Come Into the Mountains, Dear Friend
by Susan Polis Schutz
I Want to Laugh, I Want to Cry
by Susan Polis Schutz
Peace Flows from the Sky
by Susan Polis Schutz
Someone Else to Love
by Susan Polis Schutz
I'm Not That Kind of Girl
by Susan Polis Schutz
Yours If You Ask
by Susan Polis Schutz
The Best Is Yet to Be
Step to the Music You Hear, Vol. I
The Language of Friendship
The Language of Love
The Language of Happiness
The Desiderata of Happiness
by Max Ehrmann
Whatever Is, Is Best
by Ella Wheeler Wilcox
Poor Richard's Quotations
by Benjamin Franklin
I Care About Your Happiness
by Kahlil Gibran/Mary Haskell
My Life and Love Are One
by Vincent Van Gogh
I Wish You Good Spaces
by Gordon Lightfoot
We Are All Children Searching for Love
by Leonard Nimoy
Come Be with Me
by Leonard Nimoy
Creeds to Love and Live By
On the Wings of Friendship
Think of Me Kindly
by Ludwig van Beethoven
You've Got a Friend
Carole King

Catch Me with Your Smile

Peter McWilliams

Selected and arranged by
Susan Polis Schutz
with Illustrations by
Stephen Schutz

Blue Mountain Press ™.

Boulder, Colorado

Library of Congress Number: 77-84034
ISBN: 0-88396-025-7

Manufactured in the United States of America

Layout and design by SandPiper Studios, Inc.

First Printing: August, 1977
Second Printing: January, 1978
Third Printing: January, 1979

The poems included in this book have appeared earlier
in the following books by Peter McWilliams:
Love is Yes
I love therefore I am.
Evolving at the speed of love.
For Lovers and no others.
This Longing may Shorten my Life
Come Love with Me and Be My Life & Surviving
Love . . . an experience of

Information about these titles is available through
Leo Press, 5806 Elizabeth Court, Allen Park, Michigan 48101

Blue Mountain Press INC.

P.O. Box 4549, Boulder, Colorado 80306

Contents

Peter McWilliams

I must conquer my loneliness

alone.

I must be happy with myself
or I have
nothing
to offer you.

Two halves have
little choice
but to
join;
and yes,
they do
make a
whole.

but two
wholes
when they coincide . . .

that is
beauty.

that is
love.

I love you
for the love you give me.

You love me
for the love I give you.

I do not know who first gave
or who first took
or where it all began

But I am happy that it did.

I am happy that it is.

I am happy as it is.

I am in short
        in long
        in love
                (and happy!)

I don't want
to build my
life around
you,

but I want to
include you
in the building
of my life.

In those rare
moments when
all desires
have been fulfilled,

my mind
rests
on only
you.

This,
for me,
is love.

I know
    love
because
    I know
    you.

I know
    you
because
    I know
    love.

if
I give you
a reason
for loving,

I give
me
a reason
for living.

The world is good.

I feel whole & directed.

Touch my Joy with me.

I cannot keep
my smiles
in single file.

They are done.
My poems, on you, for a time, are done.
My emotions are becoming repetitive;
My poetry would soon follow suit.
At sad times I think of a sad poem.
At happy times I think of you.
At ultimate times I think of us.

And on what note should this
unfinished symphony
end?

Optimistically I see us as one.

Pessimistically I see our death.

Pessimism is the more realistic
of the two . . .
                    but
                        optimism is the way
of the love poet.

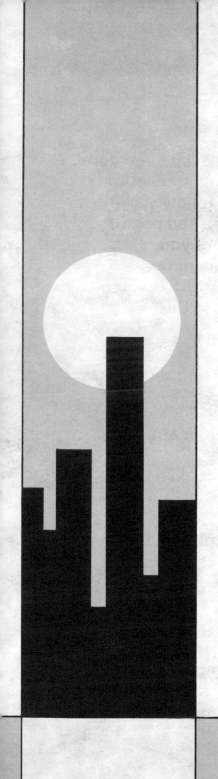

I sit
atop
the
Empire State
thinking
thoughts
of my
love
for
you.

And the
TV transmitter
above me,
with all its
millions and
billions of
kilowatts,
cannot
impress the
Universe
one million-billionth
as much
as the
love-thoughts
I
send
to
you.

writing
a poem
of our
love

is
like

coloring
a
color.

I cannot write of
      my love for you.

I cannot select the proper
  words and phrases.

I have lost my discrimination.

since you,
  everything is good.

Your Joy
is my
desire.

Your happiness
my vocation.

your fulfillment
my goal.

if you
love me,
tell me
so.

if you
tell me
love me
so.

if
All
is not
One,

at least
we
are.

you have
great power
over my love.

my love has
great power
over me.

Let's hope you
value your freedom
with me

more than you
value your
freedom
to
be free.

I am young
so love is new.

there is so much
I want to know
about you.

so many things I
want to do
with you.

So many
        embraces.

So many
        moments.

I have
no thing
to share
with you
but my
      life.

I have
no thing
to experience
with you
but our
      love.

this is all.

is all enough?

went out today
on a
busy-ness trip.

I wheeled and dealed
and smiled & beguiled
and got all I wanted.

I returned home to
find I had missed
a long distance
phone call from
you.

the trip was a failure.

missing you

could turn from

pain
to
pleasure

if only I knew

you

were missing me

too

all that is
pleasurable
will be our
domain . . .

the only
hurt will be
growing pains.

it's all new to me, too.
But I love it,

and you.

of
one
color
that best
describes
my love,

white

is my
choice,
for
white
encompasses
all
colors,

and
my
love
can
become
any
color
required
or
desired.

the red of passion

the orange of intensity

the yellow of happiness

the green of gentleness

the blue of tenderness

the purple of contentment

the gold of love

> and
> I am my
> love's prism

joy
is a word I use
to describe our
love.

love
is a word I use
to describe our
joy.

I am
in love
with you

that is

    I am in love,

    hoping you'll
    join me.

Ecstasy.

say the
word aloud:

ecstasy.

shout the
word, as
loud as
you
can:

ecstasy!

softly;
gently,
tenderly,
breathe
the word:

ecstasy.

and
this
is
my
love.

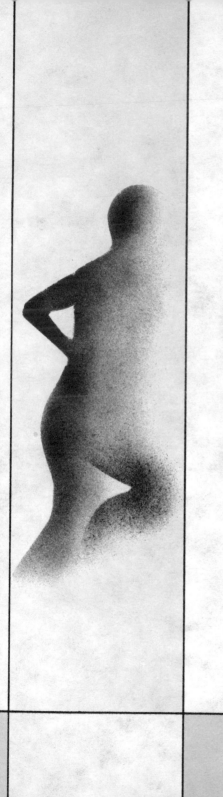

I remember thinking once
that it would be good
if you left because
then I could get some
Important Things
done.

since you've left I've done
nothing. nothing
is as important
as you.

even on the
busiest of days
I think about you
every other thought.

When we are
together
we are
one,

when we are
apart
each is
whole.

Let this be our dream;
let this be our goal.

we've both been kicking
around the universe for
some time now, alone,
and doing alright.

but somewhere in the
back of our hearts
was a tugging - - -
not a perpetual longing,
but some subtle gnawing - - -
that we might be better
with another;
not too dependent,
not too independent,
but rather like the
baby bear's porridge

                    Just Right.

I enjoy you.

your body.
your life style.
your appreciation of me.
your warmth.
your hesitancy to speak &
your freedom to touch.

In holding you I am held.

I missed you last night.
I missed you this morning.
I meditated.
I no longer miss you.
I love you.

My love is
not
a red red rose;

for red red roses
with today's advanced
methods of cross-
pollination are much
too common.

Find me a flower
that is
beguiling,
whimsical,
lyrical,
many-faceted,
perfectly imperfect,
and
one of a kind.

Give it a
name that
matches its
uniqueness

and to this
I may dare
to compare
My love.

I want to
explore the delights
of
one to one
human emotion
with you.

I want to say
whatever words
need be said
to get words
out of the way.

I am impatient.
I am frightened.
I am fascinated.
I am in love with you.

All I know is that

I love you.
I want you
Some times I need you.

You are someone
and being with you
something I
long for.

and I love you.

That's all I know

you are now
part of my life.

In all decisions
you are a consideration.

In all problems
(mostly in terms
of solution) you
are a factor.

In all Joy you are
sharing in all sorrow
support.

I love you my friend.

I am a friend to you
my love.

I am
falling faster
than I said
I would
or thought
I could . . .

you're so
comforting
&
creative
&
beautiful
&
full filling . . .

help me.
break my
fall.
catch me
    with your smile.

Afterword

This book represents the good that can happen in my life when I remain open <u>no matter what</u>. The openness referred to specifically here is letting "outsiders" tamper with my romantic poetics.

I'm a bit spoiled, you see. Partly due to self-defense but mostly due to ignorance, I began publishing my own poetry in the summer of 1967. This was the summer of love-ins and the first glimmerings of enlightenment and the sales of romantic poetry books flourished. I kept falling in love and writing about that and printing books and selling them from the back of my 1960 Ford stationwagon. I was in charge, totally, and that's what I mean when I say I'm spoiled. I had it, as the song goes, my way.

One of the first "outsiders" to contact me was Doubleday and Company. I thought "Why not jump on the Doubleday bandwagon?" so I contracted to do a book of poetry with them. Little did I know Doubleday was hoping to jump on my bandwagon, so there we were, jumping all over each other's bandwagons. Needless to say, no one had any time to sell the book. When I complained of poor sales they responded with wide-eyed innocence, "But you're outselling Yevtushenko two-to-one!" That's fine, I told them, as long as they sell half as many of my books in Russia as Yevtushenko. They didn't quite see the logic of that.

I then went to Random House. It was clear from the beginning that A Random House Was Not a Home, but we went through the ritual of lunches and conferences and offers and counter offers and tactical refusals and finally some untactical ones.

Hallmark wanted to use some of my poetry on greeting cards, but they wanted the right to do "minor rewriting." They took one of my favorite poems:

> God
> created
> all things
> but He took
> special care
> in crafting
> the rose
> and you.

This sentiment, unfortunately, did not fit any of the Hallmark Holiday Categories (Christmas, New Year's, Feast of the Circumcision, National Potato Week, etc.) so they "minorly" rewrote it to read:

> God created all things,
> but he took special care
> when he created roses
> and mothers.

Well, my mother loved it. As did my grandmother. As did most of the mothers I talked with. Why, I asked myself, should I deprive so many mothers of so much happiness next Mother's Day? And how can I possibly afford to turn down Hallmark's generous offer of $25? My muse, however, was not amused, and I said no.

The stories go on and on and this is not my autobiography. I haven't mentioned the posters or the T-shirts or the record album or the fortune cookies. (For God's sake, don't get me started on the fortune cookies!) Suffice it to say that when I kept control of a creative project it worked (sometimes) and when I gave that control away it didn't (always).

It was at a point of maximum resistance to "outsiders" that Susan Polis Schutz and Stephen Schutz, who write and illustrate for Blue Mountain Arts, asked me if I would be interested in having some of my love-thoughts added to their collection of greeting cards. My initial thought was: "Here lie the seeds of yet another disaster!" and my second thought was: "Oh, why not? But if this one doesn't work, never again!"

With appropriate thank-you's to God, I am pleased to report that it has worked out, and it has worked out better than I could have imagined. Susan bravely waded through the morass of my 600-or-so published poems and with her characteristic dedication and sensitivity selected and edited 17 bits of verbalized emotion. Stephen's brilliant illustrations often have me thinking that people are really buying the cards for his artwork and it doesn't matter in the slightest what the words say. I am convinced that Roget's Thesaurus, edited by Susan and illustrated by Stephen, would become a best-seller.

The cards were followed by their suggestion for a calendar and (by this time they had me eating out of their hand) this

book. I'm glad they asked me to supply this as it has
allowed me the opportunity to reaffirm the value of
openness in my life and the good that can flow naturally
from it.

> Keep hopin'
> and keep open
> and loves will come
> your way and you
> will go theirs.

This afterword would not be complete without the mention,
once again, of mothers. June Polis is Susan's mother and
one of the most enjoyable, loving and dynamic women I
have met. She is salesmanager at Blue Mountain Arts.
My mother is by far the best mother I have ever had and,
believing in reincarnation as I do, I know I have had several
thousand. I love her dearly. She is salesmanager for my
publishing company, Leo Press.

> God created all things,
> but he took special care
> when he created roses
> and salesmanagers.

That's a beautiful thought! Does anyone have Hallmark's
address?

Peter McWilliams
New York City
July 20, 1977